the Happy Dates BOOK

With 100 easy and affordable date night ideas, you'll never be stuck for a lover's adventure again!

SUITE BLISS PRINTABLES

ISBN: 978-0-6451799-0-3

YOUR LOVER'S
ADVENTURE STARTS HERE!

I bet you can't wait to fill this book with memories. This will soon become your most precious keepsake and make for some epic reminiscing.

These dates are easy, fun-filled, and sure to strengthen your relationship. Just follow these simple steps and you'll be raring to go:

TURN OFF YOUR PHONE AND GIVE EACH OTHER YOUR FULL ATTENTION.

ANSWER THE CONVERSATION STARTER AND EXPLORE THEM FULLY.

TAKE A HAPPY SNAP ON YOUR DATE & TAPE IT IN THE PHOTO SPACE.

UNDER THE PHOTO, WRITE YOUR DATE HIGHLIGHTS

WARNING - Be prepared to laugh, kiss, get intimate, stay up late, eat well, drink better and fall in love all over again.

RECREATE YOUR FIRST DATE

Recreate your first date. Get dressed up, choose the same restaurant, eat the same meal, kiss in the same spot and spoil each other like you're meeting for the first time.

CONVERSATION STARTER:

If you could start your own business, what would you do and why?

DATE COMPLETED: /   /

DATE HIGHLIGHTS:________________________________

____

____

____

YOUTUBE DANCE LESSON

Pick a YouTube dance tutorial together. Spend the evening learning the moves & shaking your booty.

CONVERSATION STARTER:

If you could learn any skill overnight, what would it be?

DATE COMPLETED: /   /

DATE HIGHLIGHTS:_________________________________

____

____

____

____

BUILD A LIVING ROOM FORT

Let your imagination run wild and build a cosy fort. Fill it with cushions, grab your drinks and spend the night being cute and cuddling up.

CONVERSATION STARTER:

If you were given a chance to explore the deepest oceans or ride a rocket to space, which would you choose?

DATE COMPLETED: /   /

DATE HIGHLIGHTS:_______________________

____

____

____

GO TO AN ARCADE

Embrace your inner big kid, go to your nearest arcade and try to win each other a prize. Stop for a greasy burger on your way home.

CONVERSATION STARTER:

What's your favourite stress reliever?

DATE COMPLETED: / /

DATE HIGHLIGHTS:______________________________

____

____

____

DINNER AND A MOVIE AT HOME

One decides on dinner while the other picks a movie.
Do yourselves a favour and learn how to make
caramel popcorn.

CONVERSATION STARTER:

How did your parents shape what success and failure
mean to you?

DATE COMPLETED: /   /

DATE HIGHLIGHTS:________________________

____

____

____

____

INDOOR ROCK CLIMBING

Head to your local rock-climbing centre. Come prepared with comfy clothes and a fear conquering mindset. Remember it's all mind over matter!

CONVERSATION STARTER:

What is the greatest fear you've overcome? How did it make you feel?

DATE COMPLETED: /   /

DATE HIGHLIGHTS:_______________________________

____

____

____

____

READY STEADY COOK

Using up to 10 random pantry and fridge ingredients, embark on a cook-off against each other. Choose your items wisely and assign 30 minutes in which to make it. Just like the show Ready Steady Cook, only one dish can win.

CONVERSATION STARTER:

What has been your most memorable TV show?

DATE COMPLETED: / /

DATE HIGHLIGHTS:_________________________

____

____

____

THRIFT STORE DRESS UP

Head to a thrift store & pick an outfit for your partner (don't let them see it just yet). Before going out for dinner, exchange threads and wear it all evening.

CONVERSATION STARTER:

What is a controversial opinion you have?

DATE COMPLETED: /   /

DATE HIGHLIGHTS:______________________________

____

____

____

PICNIC ON THE BEACH

Pack up your favourite snacks/drinks and head to
your local foreshore to enjoy the sunset.

CONVERSATION STARTER:

If you could learn the answer to one question about
your future, what would the question be?

DATE COMPLETED: /   /

DATE HIGHLIGHTS:_______________________________

____

____

____

____

COUPLES' DOUBLE DATE NIGHT

Grab your favourite couple and surprise them with a food and wine crawl. Choose three places you and your partner love and grab drinks and share plates at each venue.

CONVERSATION STARTER:

What benefit do you bring to the group when you hang out with friends?

DATE COMPLETED: /   /

DATE HIGHLIGHTS:

BLIND WINE AND CHEESE NIGHT

Select your favourite wines and cheeses from your local deli. Take turns feeding your partner while blindfolded and try to guess the cheese and wine combos.

CONVERSATION STARTER:

What smell or taste brings back great memories?

DATE COMPLETED: /   /

DATE HIGHLIGHTS:_______________________

____

____

____

____

PLAN A DREAM VACATION

Plan that trip you've been dying to take together. Nut out all the details, make an itinerary & a vision board (a collage of images and words). Hang up the board somewhere you will see often.

CONVERSATION STARTER:

What are five things you want to accomplish in your life?

DATE COMPLETED: /   /

DATE HIGHLIGHTS:___________________________

____

____

____

____

CREATE A SURPRISE DATE 1

One of you creates a surprise date for the other. Let them know what they should wear and don't give away any hints.

CONVERSATION STARTER:

What's the strangest movie you have ever seen?

DATE COMPLETED: /   /

DATE HIGHLIGHTS:_______________________________

____

____

____

____

CREATE A SURPRISE DATE 2

Now it's the other persons turn. Create a surprise date
and don't give away any hints except what to wear.

CONVERSATION STARTER:

What book has influenced you the most?

DATE COMPLETED: /   /

DATE HIGHLIGHTS:_______________________________

____

____

____

____

WHISKEY OR GIN TASTING

Book yourselves on a local spirit tasting. If there are none nearby, recreate one at home. Use the tasting sheet at the back of this book to guide you.

CONVERSATION STARTER:

What's your favourite memory with your mom? What's your favourite memory with your dad?

DATE COMPLETED: /   /

DATE HIGHLIGHTS:_______________________________

____

____

____

TV SHOW MARATHON

Snuggle up under a blanket on the sofa and binge a new show or your favourite series. Let UberEats be your chef tonight so you don't have to lift a finger.

CONVERSATION STARTER:

Have you ever seen something you can't explain?

DATE COMPLETED: /   /

DATE HIGHLIGHTS:_______________________________

____

____

____

GO TO YOUR LOCAL MARKET

Head to your local Sunday morning market and buy each other a surprise gift. Exchange your special gift at a cafe over a delicious breakfast.

CONVERSATION STARTER:

When you were a kid, did you feel that you fitted in?

DATE COMPLETED: / /

DATE HIGHLIGHTS:________________________

____

____

____

CREATE A COUPLE'S BUCKET LIST

Get a notebook and label it "Bucket List". Spend the night thinking of at least ten ideas and try to schedule one in for the following week.

CONVERSATION STARTER:

Presented with the opportunity to be immortal would you take it?

DATE COMPLETED: /   /

DATE HIGHLIGHTS:________________________________

____

____

____

____

WRITE LOVE NOTES TO EACH OTHER

Spend the evening writing love notes to your partner. Exchange one that night, then hide the rest around the house for them to find when they least expect it.

CONVERSATION STARTER:

Have you ever cried tears of joy?

DATE COMPLETED: /   /

DATE HIGHLIGHTS:______________________________

____

____

____

STAY IN BED ALL DAY

Put on your most luxurious bedding, cancel your plans and spend the day in bed. Think movies, chocolate, cheese burger delivery and plenty of snuggles.

CONVERSATION STARTER:

If you could change anything about the way you were raised, what would it be?

DATE COMPLETED: /   /

DATE HIGHLIGHTS:_______________________________

____

____

____

____

FANCY 'HIGH DOLLAR' DINNER

Get dressed up and treat yourselves to an
oh-my-goodness-how-much dining experience.

CONVERSATION STARTER:

Write a note to your younger self. What would you
say in under 100 words? Make sure you write it down.

DATE COMPLETED: /   /

DATE HIGHLIGHTS:_______________________________

____

____

____

CAMPING IN THE BACKYARD

Bring the camping experience to you. Make sure you come prepared, so you don't need to go into the house (well maybe just for the loo).

CONVERSATION STARTER:

How much have we changed since our first date?

DATE COMPLETED: /   /

DATE HIGHLIGHTS:______________________________

____

____

____

____

SPEND A DAY IN THE CITY

Head into the city and have fun. Go to a gallery, bookstore, record store, noodle house, rooftop bar, or anywhere else that takes your fancy.

CONVERSATION STARTER:

If you could live to be 500 years old, what other careers would you want to have?

DATE COMPLETED: / /

DATE HIGHLIGHTS:______________________

____

____

____

____

MAKE YOUR BEDROOM A HOTEL

Transform your bedroom into a romantic, luxury hotel room. Get the champagne, rose petals and candles. Make your favourite "room service" dinner and eat it in bed.

CONVERSATION STARTER:

What's the most memorable lesson you've ever learned?

DATE COMPLETED:　　/　　/

DATE HIGHLIGHTS:___________________________

____

____

____

____

MAKE A WHY I LOVE MY LIFE LIST

Pour your best wine and slice your favourite cheese. Each
write down at least 20 things you love about your life,
then share them with your partner.

CONVERSATION STARTER:

What is your most cherished childhood memory?

DATE COMPLETED: /   /

DATE HIGHLIGHTS:________________________________

____

____

____

PICNIC UNDER THE STARS

Grab a picnic blanket, play romantic music, prepare nibbles (think olives, cheese, crackers, dip, prosciutto and wine) and enjoy a night in the garden, under the stars.

CONVERSATION STARTER:

If your life was a movie or book, what would the title be?

DATE COMPLETED: /   /

DATE HIGHLIGHTS:_______________________________________

____

____

____

DOLLAR STORE GIFT EXCHANGE

Head to the dollar store, pick out three things that remind you of each other & exchange your gifts over a romantic dinner.

CONVERSATION STARTER:

What was your best birthday? What was your best birthday present?

DATE COMPLETED: /   /

DATE HIGHLIGHTS:_______________________

____

____

____

A NIGHT IN BARCELONA

Decorate your dining room in a Spanish theme, make tapas, mix sangria, learn a few Spanish phrases & listen to Gypsy Kings.

CONVERSATION STARTER:

Do you believe in fate? Or are we the controllers of our destiny?

DATE COMPLETED: /   /

DATE HIGHLIGHTS:________________________________

____

____

____

AXE THROWING

It's just what it sounds like. An instructor will teach you how to throw the axe. Come prepared for laughs, excitement, competition and plenty of adrenaline.

CONVERSATION STARTER:

Would you prefer to have high intelligence or high empathy?

DATE COMPLETED: / /

DATE HIGHLIGHTS:_______________________

____

____

____

MINI ROAD TRIP

Go on a mini road trip to a neighbouring town. Book a romantic Bed and Breakfast and be tourists for the day.

CONVERSATION STARTER:

When in your life have you felt awe?

DATE COMPLETED: /   /

DATE HIGHLIGHTS:___________________________________

____

____

____

____

TRY A COOKING CLASS

Enrol in a cooking class (face-to-face or virtual). A cooking class is the perfect way to enjoy quality time together while improving your culinary skills.

CONVERSATION STARTER:

What's the most creative thing you've ever done?

DATE COMPLETED: /   /

DATE HIGHLIGHTS:_______________________

____

____

____

BOARD GAME DATE NIGHT

Dust off your board games and have some fun. Make it sexy by kissing every time you pass GO or sink your partner's battleship.

CONVERSATION STARTER:

What is the most significant difference you feel you have made in the life of another?

DATE COMPLETED: /   /

DATE HIGHLIGHTS:_______________________________

____

____

____

____

FIND THE BEST TAPAS BAR

Your mission, should you choose to accept it, is find the best tapas bar near you. Try as many dishes as you can. Come hungry to this date.

CONVERSATION STARTER:

What's the kindest thing anyone has ever done for you?

DATE COMPLETED: / /

DATE HIGHLIGHTS:_______________________

____

____

____

GO OUT FOR GELATO

Head to your local gelato bar for your most loved ice-cream. On the way home, act like teenagers and make out in the backseat.

CONVERSATION STARTER:

What do you think love is? How would you describe your love for me?

DATE COMPLETED: /   /

DATE HIGHLIGHTS:_______________________________

____

____

____

JAZZ CLUB

Head to your local jazz club, get a front row seat,
order martinis and bop away to the beats.

CONVERSATION STARTER:

What is the biggest lie you've ever been told?

DATE COMPLETED: /   /

DATE HIGHLIGHTS:_______________________________

____

____

____

____

DIY COUPLE'S PROJECT

Go to a craft store, choose a project & create it together e.g. a comic strip of how you met, paint a scene from your life, build a frame to put a photo of you lovebirds in.

CONVERSATION STARTER:

When I was a child and thought about the future, I wanted to be...

DATE COMPLETED: / /

DATE HIGHLIGHTS:_______________________

____

____

____

AT HOME MOVIE NIGHT

Kick off your shoes, order a pizza and relax on the sofa with a movie neither of you have seen before.

CONVERSATION STARTER:

What is something popular that annoys you?

DATE COMPLETED: /   /

DATE HIGHLIGHTS:_______________________________

____

____

____

HOTEL STAY FOR THE NIGHT

Book a last-minute hotel, pack a bag and have fun! Jump on the bed, raid the mini-bar and order up a club sandwich.

CONVERSATION STARTER:

When you look in the mirror, what's the first thing you check?

DATE COMPLETED: / /

DATE HIGHLIGHTS:_________________________

____

____

____

____

COMEDY CLUB

Head to your local comedy club, order your favourite drink and get ready to laugh your socks off. See who can tell the best joke on the way there.

CONVERSATION STARTER:

What do you feel are the upsides of ageing?

DATE COMPLETED: /   /

DATE HIGHLIGHTS:____________________________

____

____

____

____

CABIN RENTAL OR CAMPING TRIP

Plan a romantic camping trip. If you're not the camping types, try a cosy cabin in the woods with a log fire and hot tub.

CONVERSATION STARTER:

What would you try to do if you couldn't fail?

DATE COMPLETED: /   /

DATE HIGHLIGHTS:___________________________

____

____

____

MINIATURE GOLF

Get your cliché date night ON and head out to mini golf. The loser pays for dinner.

CONVERSATION STARTER:

In what ways would you like to be a better person?

DATE COMPLETED: /   /

DATE HIGHLIGHTS:____________________________

____

____

____

____

AT HOME SPA NIGHT

Think massages, facials, scented candles and bubbles. Find a DIY facial recipe online and make one for each other.

CONVERSATION STARTER:

What do you still want to discover in the world?

DATE COMPLETED: /   /

DATE HIGHLIGHTS:_______________________________

____

____

____

RECORD HOW YOU FELL IN LOVE

Video record each other on how you fell in love. This one might make you cringe but it's probably going to be your most treasured keepsake, ever!

CONVERSATION STARTER:

What is the hardest thing about having children?
What mistakes do you feel many parents make?

DATE COMPLETED: /   /

DATE HIGHLIGHTS:_____________________________

____

____

____

SUNSET BIKE RIDE

Pack a picnic and take a scenic bike ride around town
to catch the sunset.

CONVERSATION STARTER:

What is the most embarrassing thing that has ever
happened to you?

DATE COMPLETED: /   /

DATE HIGHLIGHTS:_______________________________

____

____

____

____

ROMANTIC CANDLELIGHT DINNER

Turn all the lights off and cook your dinner by candlelight. Keep those candles burning all night long.

CONVERSATION STARTER:

What do you allow yourself to be idealistic about?

DATE COMPLETED: /   /

DATE HIGHLIGHTS:______________________

____

____

____

____

A NIGHT IN ITALY

Create an Italian themed dining room, make pizza dough, drink Italian wine & watch the Godfather.

CONVERSATION STARTER:

What would you do if money didn't matter?

DATE COMPLETED: /   /

DATE HIGHLIGHTS:_______________________

____

____

____

PLAY VIDEO GAMES

Let your inner kid roam free tonight and play your favourite video games.

CONVERSATION STARTER:

Design your ideal country. How would it be different from your real one?

DATE COMPLETED: /   /

DATE HIGHLIGHTS:______________________________

____

____

____

____

MARGARITA NIGHT

Get the chips, salsa and salt! Make a mega bowl of nachos and a fishbowl filled with margarita mix.

CONVERSATION STARTER:

What qualities do you wish you had that you don't?

DATE COMPLETED: /   /

DATE HIGHLIGHTS:______________________

____

____

____

____

STRAWBERRIES & BUBBLE BATH

It doesn't get any more romantic than bubbles, chocolate covered strawberries and a slippery partner.

CONVERSATION STARTER:

If you could call anyone in the world and have a conversation, who would you call?

DATE COMPLETED: /   /

DATE HIGHLIGHTS:________________________

____

____

____

FONDUE FOR TWO

Grab some cheese or chocolate (why not both?) and fondue it up with marshmallows, bread and strawberries!

CONVERSATION STARTER:

Take three minutes and tell your partner your life story in as much detail as possible.

DATE COMPLETED: /   /

DATE HIGHLIGHTS:_______________________

____

____

____

A NIGHT IN PARIS

Find a French recipe, decorate your dining room in a Paris theme, drink French wine, and talk in French accents.

CONVERSATION STARTER:

What does your own personal hell look like? How about your own personal heaven?

DATE COMPLETED: /   /

DATE HIGHLIGHTS:_______________________

____

____

____

GO TO THE PLAYGROUND

Remember the joy of swings and merry-go-rounds? Kids shouldn't get to have all the fun, right? Relive childhood memories with your partner and play until your head spins. End the night with a Happy Meal.

CONVERSATION STARTER:

Describe a memorable encounter with another culture?

DATE COMPLETED: /   /

DATE HIGHLIGHTS:______________________________

____

____

____

MAKE YOUR OWN SUSHI

It's easier than you might think. Buy a sushi kit, pour yourselves a glass of saké, and get creative with the fillings.

CONVERSATION STARTER:

What was the best invention of the last 50 years?

DATE COMPLETED: /   /

DATE HIGHLIGHTS:_______________________________

____

____

____

BOWLING DATE NIGHT

Get your cliché date night ON and head out to bowling. The loser shouts the drinks!

CONVERSATION STARTER:

What, if anything, is too serious to be joked about?

DATE COMPLETED: /   /

DATE HIGHLIGHTS:_______________________________

____

____

____

____

SCULPTING AT HOME

If you think clay modelling is just for kids, think again!
Buy some clay or a sculpting set and make things like
tea light holders, gifts, pots, and love signs. Don't
forget to buy paint to make them look pretty.

CONVERSATION STARTER:

If you had magical powers to improve people around
you, what would you change about them?

DATE COMPLETED: /   /

DATE HIGHLIGHTS:_______________________________

____

____

____

____

MAKE COCKTAILS AT HOME

Knock up your favourite cocktails or find some you've never even heard of to make together.

CONVERSATION STARTER:

You must relive one day of your life forever. Which day do you choose?

DATE COMPLETED: / /

DATE HIGHLIGHTS:

GO TO A SKATING RINK

Whether you can or can't skate, head to the rink to practice or show off your mad skills!

CONVERSATION STARTER:

What have you ever learnt from a child?

DATE COMPLETED: / /

DATE HIGHLIGHTS:______________________

____

____

____

____

BAKE COOKIES TOGETHER

Find a delicious cookie recipe online (the chunkier and gooier, the better). Undo your belt, throw on Netflix and munch together.

CONVERSATION STARTER:

Do you think your dreams have meaning?

DATE COMPLETED: / /

DATE HIGHLIGHTS:_______________________

____

____

____

____

COOK A THREE COURSE DINNER

Decide on the courses together, get your apron on and hit the kitchen for some fun partner time. If you're brave enough - cook in just your apron.

CONVERSATION STARTER:

Time freezes for everyone but you for one day. What do you do?

DATE COMPLETED: /   /

DATE HIGHLIGHTS:________________________

____

____

____

PLANT A GARDEN

Make a beautiful herb & veggie patch. Pick five plants each and get your hands dirty. Research what is growing well in your climate and season. Bonus points if you can grow herbs to use for your next date night dinner.

CONVERSATION STARTER:

What consumes the bulk of your thoughts?

DATE COMPLETED: / /

DATE HIGHLIGHTS:______________________________

____

____

____

AT HOME PAINTING CLASS

Grab some blank canvases, brushes and paints. Paint each other a mini masterpiece. No skill required for this one. The more abstract - the better!

CONVERSATION STARTER:

What shaped your attitudes to money? What suspicions do you have of the very rich?

DATE COMPLETED: / /

DATE HIGHLIGHTS:________________________

____

____

____

TRILOGY MOVIE MARATHON

We're talking Star Wars, Lord of the Rings, Back to the Future - whatever takes your fancy, get ready for a dedicated night to your favourite trilogy.

CONVERSATION STARTER:

If you were to write a book, what would it be about?

DATE COMPLETED: / /

DATE HIGHLIGHTS:_______________________

____

____

____

VOLUNTEER TOGETHER

Find a place you can volunteer together and spend a day/evening giving back to your community.

CONVERSATION STARTER:

What will the future of education look like?

DATE COMPLETED: /   /

DATE HIGHLIGHTS:______________________________

____

____

____

BUILD AN ICE CREAM SUNDAE

Go wild with the toppings and make your own ice cream sundae. For each topping your partner uses, you must give them a kiss.

CONVERSATION STARTER:

What's another career that you think you would love?

DATE COMPLETED: / /

DATE HIGHLIGHTS:_______________________________

____

____

____

____

GO FISHING TOGETHER

Hire some fishing gear and try catch your dinner. Take comfy camping chairs, beers, and music for added fun.

CONVERSATION STARTER:

When do you want to retire? What do you want to do when you retire?

DATE COMPLETED: / /

DATE HIGHLIGHTS:_______________________

____

____

____

GO CANOEING OR KAYAKING

If your city allows for such an activity, go and have fun on the water. If you don't have access to this, why not go mountain biking instead?

CONVERSATION STARTER:

What are your three favourite things about me?

DATE COMPLETED: /   /

DATE HIGHLIGHTS:_______________________________

____

____

____

PROGRESSIVE DINNER

Go to three different venues for your pre-drinks, mains, and dessert. Or you can do this with friends and all host a course in your homes.

CONVERSATION STARTER:

Describe what you were feeling on our very first date?

DATE COMPLETED: /   /

DATE HIGHLIGHTS:______________________________

____

____

____

____

VISIT A FREE MUSEUM

Even if museums aren't normally your thing, you're bound to learn something new about your partner's interests.

CONVERSATION STARTER:

Who is your greatest hero?

DATE COMPLETED: / /

DATE HIGHLIGHTS:_______________________

____

____

____

____

GO CAMPING INDOORS

Put up your tent or build one out of sheets. Bonus points for putting fairy lights around your tent and making it romantic.

CONVERSATION STARTER:

What's the greatest risk you've ever taken?

DATE COMPLETED: /   /

DATE HIGHLIGHTS:______________________________

____

____

____

PLAY HOOKY FROM WORK

Call in sick and go on an adventure day together. Just make sure you don't get caught.

CONVERSATION STARTER:

Deja-vu: is there anything to it or merely coincidence?

DATE COMPLETED: / /

DATE HIGHLIGHTS:________________________________

____

____

____

GAMES NIGHT WITH FRIENDS

Dust off the poker set and host a games night. Or host a virtual games night with friends across the globe.

CONVERSATION STARTER:

Has a podcast ever had such a profound effect on you that you've changed the way you live your life?

DATE COMPLETED: /   /

DATE HIGHLIGHTS:__________________________

____

____

____

____

GO TO A WORKOUT CLASS

Couples that sweat together, stay together (is that a saying? Who cares! Give this one a go).

CONVERSATION STARTER:

If you could take us anywhere in the world right now, where would you take us?

DATE COMPLETED: /   /

DATE HIGHLIGHTS:_______________________________

____

____

____

____

BEER TASTING

Go to a local brewery or bring the brewery to you with a selection of different beers. Use the tasting sheet at the back of this book to guide you.

CONVERSATION STARTER:

What are your goals for the next two years?

DATE COMPLETED: /   /

DATE HIGHLIGHTS:________________________

____

____

____

____

SKETCH EACH OTHER NUDE

Don't worry about whether you're good at drawing, just get a sketch pad and draw. Feel free to be as abstract as you like. Be sure to frame your masterpiece.

CONVERSATION STARTER:

Which of my quirks do you love the most?

DATE COMPLETED: /   /

DATE HIGHLIGHTS:_______________________________________

____

____

____

____

ORDER FOR EACH OTHER

Head to your favourite restaurant and instead of picking what you want to eat, pick something for your partner to eat.

CONVERSATION STARTER:

What are five things you are grateful for?

DATE COMPLETED: /   /

DATE HIGHLIGHTS:______________________________

____

____

____

____

DRESS UP FOR A NIGHT IN

Get your fanciest outfits on, spritz your favourite perfume, talk in posh accents. cook a decadent dinner and pretend you're at the swishest place in town.

CONVERSATION STARTER:

What do you think about when you are by yourself?

DATE COMPLETED: /   /

DATE HIGHLIGHTS:_______________________________

____

____

____

PLAY TRUTH OR DARE

Have some fun and play truth or dare. If you're feeling a bit spicy, Google the sexy dice game for some intimate couple's fun.

CONVERSATION STARTER:

What is the weirdest thing about you?

DATE COMPLETED: / /

DATE HIGHLIGHTS:_______________________

____

____

____

____

TRY A NEW GROUPON

Pick a fun Groupon activity that you normally wouldn't
be interested in and give it a go.

CONVERSATION STARTER:

If you had the ability to erase something that you did
in the past, what would it be?

DATE COMPLETED: /   /

DATE HIGHLIGHTS:________________________________

____

____

____

____

MAKE A TIME CAPSULE

Get a shoebox and fill it with keepsakes, cards, photos, movie stubs etc. Include a letter to your future self. Decide on a specific date you'll open the box in 10 years' time.

CONVERSATION STARTER:

Does your job make you happy?

DATE COMPLETED: /   /

DATE HIGHLIGHTS:_______________________________

____

____

____

MAKE A PLAYLIST OF SONGS

Use Spotify to make a playlist that reminds you of your partner. Bop away to it over dinner and drinks.

CONVERSATION STARTER:

What's one thing you wish you knew how to do?

DATE COMPLETED: /   /

DATE HIGHLIGHTS:_______________________

____

____

____

____

COUPLES' PERSONALITY QUIZ

Google "couple's quiz" and take your pick from the huge selection. The 16 personalities quiz, the 5 love languages and the enneagram are all amazing.

CONVERSATION STARTER:

Do you usually achieve the goals you set? Why or why not?

DATE COMPLETED: /   /

DATE HIGHLIGHTS:______________________

____

____

____

PYJAMA PARTY

Choose the movie, get the popcorn popping and slip into your pyjamas. Bonus points if you and your partners PJs match.

CONVERSATION STARTER:

Have you ever had dreams about a past life?

DATE COMPLETED: /   /

DATE HIGHLIGHTS:___________________

____

____

____

WATCH THE SUNRISE & GO FOR BREAKFAST

Get up early and watch the sunrise. Treat yourselves to a cafe breakfast afterward.

CONVERSATION STARTER:

Do you believe in extra-terrestrial life? Elaborate why?

DATE COMPLETED: /   /

DATE HIGHLIGHTS:________________________

____

____

____

GO TO HOME OPENS FOR FUN

This one's fun if you like looking at how other people live. Who knows, maybe you'll find your dream home!

CONVERSATION STARTER:

Do you believe in other dimensions and parallel universes?

DATE COMPLETED: /   /

DATE HIGHLIGHTS:________________________

____

____

____

START A COOKBOOK TOGETHER

Spend your evening writing down all your favourite recipes in a blank journal. Who knows, maybe you'll end up self-publishing this on Amazon!

CONVERSATION STARTER:

What scene in a movie has evoked the most feelings out of you?

DATE COMPLETED: / /

DATE HIGHLIGHTS:_______________________

____

____

____

____

WINE TASTING

Go to a local winery or bring the winery to you with a selection of wines. Use the tasting sheet at the back of this book to guide you.

CONVERSATION STARTER:

If past lives are real, what was yours?

DATE COMPLETED: / /

DATE HIGHLIGHTS:_______________________

____

____

____

____

START A CONVERSATION WITH A COUPLE AT A BAR

Throw down a shot of courage and strike up a conversation with another couple. Who knows, you might meet lifelong friends.

CONVERSATION STARTER:
What is the craziest thing you want to achieve?

DATE COMPLETED: /   /

DATE HIGHLIGHTS:______________________________________

____

____

____

DEGUSTATION DINNER

This is a must do. A degustation dinner is a large selection of dishes paired with wine. Wear stretchy pants.

CONVERSATION STARTER:

What makes you feel the most loved?

DATE COMPLETED: /   /

DATE HIGHLIGHTS:_______________________________

____

____

____

____

WRITE A MINI STORY

Take turns writing a sentence until you have a complete story. Getting creative together is a great bonding activity.

CONVERSATION STARTER:

What's the most spontaneous thing you've done lately? What is the craziest thing you've ever done, and would you do it again?

DATE COMPLETED: /   /

DATE HIGHLIGHTS:_______________________________

____

____

____

____

GO ON A HIKE TOGETHER

Long or short, it doesn't matter, getting out into the great outdoors will make you both feel good. Plus, a good walk warrants a pub lunch afterward, right?   .

CONVERSATION STARTER:

If you could see into the future, what would you want to know?

DATE COMPLETED: /   /

DATE HIGHLIGHTS:_______________________

____

____

____

____

SEXY DRESS UP & ROLE PLAY

Try this intimate date night and see what happens. Try role play or ask your partner what they'd like you to wear.

CONVERSATION STARTER:

What is your love language? Take the online quiz if you don't know.

DATE COMPLETED: / /

DATE HIGHLIGHTS:_______________________

____

____

____

ESCAPE ROOM

Come prepared with your sharpest detective skills. Work together using your complementing skills to escape.

CONVERSATION STARTER:

Can you think of a piece of technology that's made the world worse? How about a piece of technology that's made the world better?

DATE COMPLETED: /   /

DATE HIGHLIGHTS:______________________________

____

____

____

____

GO-KARTS

Whether you like Formula 1 or not, head to your local go-karting joint and race for the bragging rights of "best go-karter".

CONVERSATION STARTER:

What is the scariest thing you've ever done?

DATE COMPLETED: / /

DATE HIGHLIGHTS:________________________________

____

____

____

ENJOY A BOOZY BRUNCH

Go and enjoy a boozy brunch guilt free. It's 5pm somewhere, right? Bonus if you can find a bottomless brunch.

CONVERSATION STARTER:

Would you go on the first passenger flight to Mars?

DATE COMPLETED: /   /

DATE HIGHLIGHTS:_______________________________

____

____

____

____

JAPANESE TAKEAWAY NIGHT

Did someone say sashimi? Get the chopsticks out and indulge in your favourite Japanese.

CONVERSATION STARTER:

Will technology save humanity or destroy it?

DATE COMPLETED: /   /

DATE HIGHLIGHTS:_______________________________

____

____

____

____

GO ON A RIVER CRUISE

If your city has one, book yourselves on a river cruise
or sightseeing bus and be tourists for the day.

CONVERSATION STARTER:

Talk about some of the interesting people you have
met in your lifetime?

DATE COMPLETED: /   /

DATE HIGHLIGHTS:_______________________________

____

____

____

HOST A DATE NIGHT WITH FRIENDS

Get your best friends over and host a dinner date. Get them to bring a plate or if you're feeling generous, cook them a meal.

CONVERSATION STARTER:

What book has changed one of your long-held opinions?

DATE COMPLETED: /   /

DATE HIGHLIGHTS:________________________________

____

____

____

____

SPA DATE - COUPLE'S MASSAGE

For an indulgent date, head to the spa for a couple's massage. Get ready to be super relaxed and blissful.

CONVERSATION STARTER:

What quote resonates with you more than any other?

DATE COMPLETED: /   /

DATE HIGHLIGHTS:_______________________________________

____

____

____

____

BEER TASTING NOTES

BEER NAME: _______________

Aroma: ⬡ ⬡ ⬡ ⬡ ⬡
Appearance: ⬡ ⬡ ⬡ ⬡ ⬡
Taste: ⬡ ⬡ ⬡ ⬡ ⬡
Finish: ⬡ ⬡ ⬡ ⬡ ⬡

Overall Score: 1　2　3　4　5

BEER NAME: _______________

Aroma: ⬡ ⬡ ⬡ ⬡ ⬡
Appearance: ⬡ ⬡ ⬡ ⬡ ⬡
Taste: ⬡ ⬡ ⬡ ⬡ ⬡
Finish: ⬡ ⬡ ⬡ ⬡ ⬡

Overall Score: 1　2　3　4　5

BEER NAME: _______________

Aroma: ⬡ ⬡ ⬡ ⬡ ⬡
Appearance: ⬡ ⬡ ⬡ ⬡ ⬡
Taste: ⬡ ⬡ ⬡ ⬡ ⬡
Finish: ⬡ ⬡ ⬡ ⬡ ⬡

Overall Score: 1　2　3　4　5

BEER NAME: _______________

Aroma: ⬡ ⬡ ⬡ ⬡ ⬡
Appearance: ⬡ ⬡ ⬡ ⬡ ⬡
Taste: ⬡ ⬡ ⬡ ⬡ ⬡
Finish: ⬡ ⬡ ⬡ ⬡ ⬡

Overall Score: 1　2　3　4　5

BEER NAME: _______________

Aroma: ⬡ ⬡ ⬡ ⬡ ⬡
Appearance: ⬡ ⬡ ⬡ ⬡ ⬡
Taste: ⬡ ⬡ ⬡ ⬡ ⬡
Finish: ⬡ ⬡ ⬡ ⬡ ⬡

Overall Score: 1　2　3　4　5

BEER NAME: _______________

Aroma: ⬡ ⬡ ⬡ ⬡ ⬡
Appearance: ⬡ ⬡ ⬡ ⬡ ⬡
Taste: ⬡ ⬡ ⬡ ⬡ ⬡
Finish: ⬡ ⬡ ⬡ ⬡ ⬡

Overall Score: 1　2　3　4　5

WHISKEY TASTING NOTES

NAME: _______________

Type: _______________

Proof/Age: _______________

Aroma: ⬡ ⬡ ⬡ ⬡ ⬡
Taste: ⬡ ⬡ ⬡ ⬡ ⬡

Score: 1 2 3 4 5

NAME: _______________

Type: _______________

Proof/Age: _______________

Aroma: ⬡ ⬡ ⬡ ⬡ ⬡
Taste: ⬡ ⬡ ⬡ ⬡ ⬡

Score: 1 2 3 4 5

NAME: _______________

Type: _______________

Proof/Age: _______________

Aroma: ⬡ ⬡ ⬡ ⬡ ⬡
Taste: ⬡ ⬡ ⬡ ⬡ ⬡

Score: 1 2 3 4 5

NAME: _______________

Type: _______________

Proof/Age: _______________

Aroma: ⬡ ⬡ ⬡ ⬡ ⬡
Taste: ⬡ ⬡ ⬡ ⬡ ⬡

Score: 1 2 3 4 5

NAME: _______________

Type: _______________

Proof/Age: _______________

Aroma: ⬡ ⬡ ⬡ ⬡ ⬡
Taste: ⬡ ⬡ ⬡ ⬡ ⬡

Score: 1 2 3 4 5

NAME: _______________

Type: _______________

Proof/Age: _______________

Aroma: ⬡ ⬡ ⬡ ⬡ ⬡
Taste: ⬡ ⬡ ⬡ ⬡ ⬡

Score: 1 2 3 4 5

WINE TASTING NOTES

WINE TYPE: _______________

Aroma:
Appearance:
Taste:
Finish:

Overall Score: 1 2 3 4 5

WINE TYPE: _______________

Aroma:
Appearance:
Taste:
Finish:

Overall Score: 1 2 3 4 5

WINE TYPE: _______________

Aroma:
Appearance:
Taste:
Finish:

Overall Score: 1 2 3 4 5

WINE TYPE: _______________

Aroma:
Appearance:
Taste:
Finish:

Overall Score: 1 2 3 4 5

WINE TYPE: _______________

Aroma:
Appearance:
Taste:
Finish:

Overall Score: 1 2 3 4 5

WINE TYPE: _______________

Aroma:
Appearance:
Taste:
Finish:

Overall Score: 1 2 3 4 5

THANK YOU
FOR YOUR PURCHASE

I've been happy dancing since I heard you bought my book! I hope as a couple you've discovered a little more about each other whilst having fun and getting frisky!

I'm Steph, the gal behind Suite Bliss Printables. If you've enjoyed this book, I would LOVE IT if you could leave me a review on Amazon.

Happy Dating!

big love
Steph

SUITE BLISS PRINTABLES

Printed in Great Britain
by Amazon

20553182R00061